WIZARDRY

for the Uninitiated

WIZARDRY

for the Uninitiated

By

Thea Faye

Published by Avalonia

BM Avalonia
London
WC1N 3XX
England, UK

www.avaloniabooks.co.uk

WIZARDRY FOR THE UNINITIATED

ISBN (10) 1-905297-13-0
ISBN (13) 978-1-905297-13-9

FIRST EDITION, 2007
Design by Satori
Illustrations & Photography by Thea Faye, Aleq Grai or as credited

About Thea Faye

Thea Faye is an initiate of the Mysteries and has studied many different branches of magick over the years. The question of what are witches and wizards is one which has intrigued her all her life, inspiring her to embark on a quest to determine what differences, if any, there are between the two traditions. The results of her work you hold in your hands.

Thea lives with her husband and their three small children, 5 cats, an aviary of birds otherwise known as *CatTV* and a rabbit called Bunny.

On a more personal note, thanks need to be made to Aleq Grai who has proven a worthy adversary for quite some time now, the Avalonia forums for the impetus to put pen to paper and Owen for demonstrating what a proper little wizard should be.

You are welcome to write to the Author:

Thea Faye

c/o BM Avalonia, London, WC1N 3XX, United Kingdom

You can also contact her through www.avaloniabooks.co.uk

Dedication

To my first teacher Marian Green.

Because when you do the Work you end up in unexpected places .

Index

Wizardry for the Uninitiated

"There is reality and there is fantasy;
the real magick trick lies in knowing which is which."
Zern the Wizard

Once solely concerned with the realms of spiritual evolution and awareness, modern day magick in its bastardised form is an increasingly profitable business and it appears that even oaths sworn to your Gods can be tossed aside when there is money to be made. In a world where families cannot wait to read the latest Harry Potter novel and shows like *Buffy the Vampire Slayer* and *Charmed* attract bigger and bigger audiences, the spotlight has inevitably turned to the question of magick in the real world and whether it is truly possible to initiate yourself into the mysteries of a magickal life. Do witches really exist? Are there real vampires lurking in dark alleys? Whatever happened to the fairies at the bottom of the garden? And for every one of the questions, there are countless books all professing to provide that answer, of course, being a resounding 'they're here!' It should come as no surprise that telling people what they want to hear is a sure-fire way of selling your message.

No longer confined to the worthy, the hard working, the elite, these days, no bookshop is complete without a well stocked non-fiction section on magick in its various guises. From the realms of dragons, druids and angels to the more prosaic spell books with incantations for any result the aspiring witch could desire, everything you could possibly need to know can be yours for the sake of a few pounds – or so the authors would have you believe. Gardner did an admirable job in bringing witchcraft to the masses through his initiatory system known as Wicca, however over the brief few decades since he first established it, increasing numbers of outsiders have looked at his rituals and techniques and interpreted them to suit themselves without necessarily first obtaining a full understanding of their symbolism and purpose and now the lines are blurred between those who have a genuine understanding of what he had to teach and those who are in it solely for the T-shirt, as the secrets of the inner mysteries are supposedly laid bare for all to see, regardless of whether they work to deserve them or not. Too many oath breakers have failed to keep silent and handed out the rituals to all and sundry so that now it can be hard to tell who are the true initiates and who are simply the wannabe poseurs or worse, the more sinister predators utilising the mystique and kudos of the Wiccan priesthood to have their wicked way.

Yet for all the searchlights and attempts to penetrate the hidden depths by the profane, wizardry has thus far managed to remain in the shadows, as those of us fortunate to be steeped in the teachings of

Merlin and his descendants have continued with our work, quietly, without fanfare, for if we were to advertise the true secrets of our success, we would cease to hold the esteemed positions in society we do (and believe me, there is no such thing as an unsuccessful wizard. We are lawyers, politicians, doctors, teachers, professors, business professionals and yes, even authors). It is one thing to obtain high office through hard work or even right of birth; it is quite another to allegedly cheat by using magickal means to obtain the same ends (regardless of the fact that magick requires just as much work as any other method).

So why am I choosing to break the bonds of secrecy and reveal all to the world? It is very simple. I have been hearing increasing cries of *"why can I not find any information on wizardry? I want to be a wizard!"* The only way to counter the work of the infidel is to be there to make sure the information that is available to the would be wizard of today is genuine, fact based and sound so that those who study it are truly worthy of the title. Combine that with the reality that there are no oaths per se, more a wizard code of honour not to reveal our methods to those who do not deserve them, it is an unpalatable truth to some that if you do not understand, no amount of explanation on my part will enable you to unlock the doors to the Tower until such a time when you are ready. In reading this you automatically reveal your desire to be worthy, although time will tell whether you are willing to put in the work to support this wish. And so, only those who are capable of appreciating the full extent of what is to be revealed within these pages will learn the arcane lore and in so doing, by definition prove themselves deserving. Thus the secrets remain hidden in plain sight and no honour is lost.

Make no mistake. The way of the wizard is not an easy one. It involves hard work and dedication and few are of the required standard to make the grade, of which there is only one. You are either a wizard or you are not. There is no try. Yet the rewards are many to those who commit themselves. If you conquer the requisite skills, your name will be known and you will stand among the giants who have lead us to where we are today. You will achieve true immortality, for you will have left your mark indelibly upon the world. You will go further than you ever thought could be possible and then further still, for you will discover what you are truly capable of.

In this book you will find no spells, no rituals, no so-called Wheel of the Year, no talk of initiation or self dedication. Neither will this book tell you what you need to do to master the requisite skills, although it will discuss their theory in depth and the reasons why they are necessary, as well as provide you with signposts for where to turn to take the next step, for if you are serious about becoming a wizard, you will not need this book to spoon feed you. You will be not only willing, but capable, of discovering for yourself what it is you need to know.

There are also many pitfalls and dead ends, for only those who are able to recognise these for what they truly are will be worthy of the title. But if you are determined to do the work and follow the guidelines herein to their logical conclusion, then, my friend, you truly will be a WIZARD.

The Men & Myths of Wizardry

Terry Pratchett once wrote in *Soul Music* that the term wizard is derived from *"the old Wys-ars, lit. one who, at bottom, is very smart."* Phnar, phnar, as they say. Yet, as is so often the way, this definition is one which holds more truth than might at first appear to the casual reader. Of course, we all know that the word actually derives from *"wise man"* (wys-ard c.1400-50) and referred specifically to men who had mastered a vast array of magickal techniques and skills, although in these supposedly enlightened times, there is no need to be bound by gender any more. They may currently be in the minority, but women too can be wizards. It is for this reason that wizards are referred to as male throughout this text, but it should be taken as read that this is equally applicable to women who choose to study the techniques of this path, there being no female version of the noun, just as a male witch is still a witch, not a warlock and certainly not to be confused with a wizard. The skill- and mindset of a wizard is very different to that required by witchcraft or the so-called religion of the witches, Wicca.

So let us make one thing very, very clear. A wizard is not a Wiccan, whether initiated or not, although there would be nothing to stop one training in the other tradition. A wizard is not a witch. Wizardry is not Wicca. Wizardry is not witchcraft. Nor do wizards work with archetypes or worship the God and Goddess(TM) and anyone who tells you that wizards do really should be asking themselves when and where exactly the concept of an unnamed, generic Goddess and Her consort came from. Indeed, just as you do not need to work with deities to practise witchcraft, neither do you need to involve yourself with Them Upstairs if you wish to become a wizard. Wizardry is not a religion, it is a magickal system and worship or obeisance to a Higher Being plays no part in it. As the infamous Crowley put it, *"there is no God but Man"*. This is not to say that wizards do not ever involve themselves with the Gods, but you will find that those who do, work with specific deities for specific purposes and frequently devote themselves to a particular patron, building a long and intimate relationship with their God over the course of a lifetime. However, for the most part, we do not trouble them and they do not trouble us (and it is interesting to note that one of the most famous religious texts, the Bible, tells us that the Christian God specifically prohibits witchcraft but has no problem with wizardry. In fact, He actively helps to teach wizardry to Man).

However, being a wizard requires more than wisdom. In accordance with the Maxim of the Magus, it is all very well and good to Know; you also need to be willing to Dare, to put your studies into practise.

There is a certain *je ne sais quoi* about the *"wys-ars"* which lower mortals have mistakenly confused with arrogance and smugness. Unfortunately, when you know just how much any individual is capable of, that this is more than most believe and that, indeed, you have seen, experienced and understood more about the workings of the universe than the majority of people will see in their entire lives, it can be difficult to dumb down so as not to appear too much out of place, which is one reason why those wizards who have travelled a long way down their path increasingly retreat to their Tower where they do not have to bother making the effort and can devote themselves to further study. Moreover, one might say that it is impossible to ever fully return to the world of ordinary mortals when you have learned how to interpret the dawn chorus, dined with the Queen of the Fey, discussed philosophy with angels and demons and commanded lightning to strike where you will, and done so to such an extent that it is commonplace, nothing more than everyday living to you. It is not for nothing that Carveth Read wrote in his article The Mind of the Wizard: *"the professional wizard is one whom others ask to help them because they believe that he has the knack of it"*[1]

Whilst they might not be able to pinpoint exactly why, people are drawn to wizards to solve their problems because they believe they

[1] British Journal of Psychology, October 1918

will succeed where others have failed. Indeed, Read even goes so far as to say *"As a tribal initiation separates a man from the women and boys, so the wizard's initiation makes him a 'superman' ... He becomes necessary in every crisis of life, at birth and marriage, in misfortune, sickness and death."* No wonder many eventually retire to their Towers – the demands on your time to fix every little thing can become time consuming if you are not careful and being a *'superman'* people find it difficult to comprehend that wizards too need a break.

The way of the wizard is ancient indeed. For those who believe that Christians are anti-magick, it may well be surprising to learn that tales of wizardry can be found in the Bible not to mention even earlier myths. A detailed analysis of Biblical attitudes towards magick in general is a subject fit to fill volumes all by itself, but nevertheless, we can begin our examination of wizardry through the ages by looking at how it is depicted in the tale of Moses, one of the first wizards.

Moses

There can be no doubt that Moses was an extremely gifted wizard and one who appears to have had an especial affinity with the element of water. The parting of the Red Sea alone is an impeccable demonstration of his abilities in its impressive mastery of the tides. He also worked with water when he produced it from a rock at a time when his people were suffering from thirst, sweetened bitter water to make it drinkable and was seen to turn it into blood on another occasion. There can be no doubt that Moses was an expert at elemental manipulation and whilst over the ages it has become prudent to be a little more circumspect, in his day, was able to show off his skills when and as needed without fear of retribution, due in no small part to the fact that he was acting under the auspices and direct command of his God.

However, these are not the only occasions on which Moses performed wonders. He worked with serpents more than once, unsurprising given their strong connections with knowledge, power and magick. There was the occasion when he threw a rod to the ground, on God's command, for it to become a snake and then picked it up whereupon it became a rod again. God also gave Moses instructions on how to deal with snakes when he assisted him in creating an enchanted statue which could cure snake bites. It is not unreasonable to surmise that the tales recounted in the Bible are merely the more impressive ones, worthy of note because they marked key events in his story – one suspects that these were only a small part of Moses' magickal prowess and there is a theory that he was well schooled in Egyptian magick during his time in the court of Pharoah.

The tale of Moses is an interesting one in many ways, not least of which because it demonstrates that whilst it is impossible to be a Christian witch and still be acceptable to your God (Exodus 22:18 amongst other verses), it is more than possible to be a Christian wizard. Indeed, not only is it allowable under God's laws, it is even possible to learn techniques and skills from your God. The Bible is full of wizardry if you look – the Battle of Jericho was won by magickal means, for example. However, and here is the critical piece of information, if you choose to be a Christian wizard, you must take care to always pay homage to the ultimate source of your power, your God, lest you face dire consequences (Deuteronomy 32:51). It is for this reason that many wizards prefer not to mix religion with magick – there is nothing you can get from a god that you cannot master for yourself if you are willing to put in the time and effort and doing it for yourself is ultimately less complicated than permanently tying yourself in subservience to a higher being.

The techniques which Moses used are ones which are commonplace amongst the modern wizard and rumours abound of wizards who have attempted to recreate these feats to impress their friends with their abilities only to have success beyond their expectations, innocents dying in the process. An in depth understanding of the four elements is key to many magickal practises and, once having built an understanding and relationship with the elements, it is a small step to being able to command them to your will. Any modern day wizard should at the very least be able to demonstrate an understanding of the theory behind everything Moses did, even if parting the seas is out of the reach of all but the most adept of masters. Plus, of course, there is the fact that just because you can do something doesn't mean that you should. Moses had good reason to do what he did; it is questionable whether anyone today would have the same motivation, let alone the understanding of the impact such an undertaking would have on the environment.

Merlin

No examination of the history of wizardry would be complete without the greatest and most famous wizard of all time, none other than Merlin. As with many magickal, mythical heroes, his birth was otherworldly, being the son of an incubus and a human, thus born with magick running through his veins and those who claim to be of wizard blood allege they can trace their lineage back to him.

Best known as Arthur's closest adviser and friend, Merlin was Welsh and tales of his knowledge and prowess can be found throughout Welsh folklore. He was a bard, wise man and prophet. Legend has him responsible for many great acts which had a huge impact on the course of British history, including the engineering of Stonehenge which even now exerts a great force on the British psyche, not to mention creating the opportunity for Uther Pendragon to father Arthur, the greatest King Britain has ever known and one who is only sleeping, and who will, according to the lore, return whenever the land has need of him.

Merlin was the basis for many famous epic poems, including those by Geoffrey of Monmouth and Robert de Boron and it is worth noting that de Boron has Merlin receiving some of his powers and knowledge from the Christian God, again serving as a further reminder that wizardry is perfectly acceptable in His eyes. Merlin can be held to be the quintessence of wizardry; realistically, the character we know and love today is most likely to be a composite of various stories and legends, compressed and combined over the centuries until what we are left with is what our society and culture believes a wizard ought to be and should represent. As such, looking to Merlin is an extremely good guide as to what any potential should aspire to be. However, I should caveat that with a warning to take care not to confuse the romantic fantasy with the mundane reality (especially since in any case the latter is frequently more fantastical than any story teller can weave).

Alessandro di Cagliostro

(or Giuseppe Balsamo)

Cagliostro is famous to us through many works of fiction, including those of Dumas, who took inspiration from his life for his *Memoirs of a Physician,* Robert Anton Wilson, who referenced him in his *The Historical Illuminatus Chronicles* and Umberto Eco, who often mentions him in *Foucault's Pendulum.* A real person, his true name is generally believed to be Guiseppe Balsamo. He was an initiate into

Freemasonry, as well as the Sovereign Military Order of the Knights of Malta and founded the Egyptian Rite of Freemasonry in the Hague. Alas, he appears to have placed too much emphasis on the wizardly arts of trickery and deception, being an accomplished forger and was prosecuted in the affair of the diamond necklace, although he was eventually acquitted and asked to leave France. He was eventually captured by the Inquisition and sentenced to death for being a Mason, although his sentence was later commuted to life imprisonment.

Nicholas Flamel

Another wizard whose fame has spread into the realms of the layman due to his being cited in many works of fiction. Much speculation and rumour surround him, but one thing is certain – he is considered to be an important figure in occult history because he is held to have discovered the Philosopher's Stone (or, to be more precise, rediscovered the secret, having translated a mysterious short book full of alchemical symbols and arcane mysteries) and thus knew the method of how to turn base metals into precious ones. He and his wife, Perenelle, were also alleged to have discovered the secret of immortality and certainly he successfully ensured that his name would be known long after his remains were dust.

Heinrich Cornelius Agrippa

Agrippa left his mark on the magickal world with his masterpiece, *Three Books Of Occult Philosophy*. More circumspect than the average wizard, he spent most of his life working on theories of magick and theological conundrums and although one might expect this to have lead to all sorts of persecution and litigation, went through his life relatively unscathed by accusations of heresy or any form of persecution. His published works still form an integral part of any serious wizard's library.

Faust

Although Dr Faust is popular as a literary figure made famous by the likes of Goethe and Marlowe, Johann Georg Faust was an actual person who was a very traditional wizard and alchemist. Like many masters of magick, he knew the art of invisibility well and so we know little about him (since invisibility covers more than the mere act of remaining physically hidden), although there are stories of the devil accompanying him in the form of a black dog (a traditional wizard familiar). His skill at divination was superb and his ability to summon spirits was such that he was reputedly able to conjure up ancient heroes for an audience of his students.

Scott Cunningham, Stewart Farrar, Gerald Gardner & Alex Sanders

It is a myth that any of these men were wizards. They were all famous Wiccans.

Oberon Zell-Ravenheart

His sense of humour, if nothing else, certainly qualifies Zell-Ravenheart as a wizard in the modern sense of the word.

Derren Brown

Derren Brown repeatedly states that there is no psychism or *"real"* magick in what he does and although many, many people refuse to believe him, he is telling the truth. So why, then, does he merit inclusion in a list of genuine wizards? Because he is highly skilled at what he does. He is an absolute master of many techniques of mental manipulation which are extremely useful to any wizard. Study his work well; if you know what you are looking for, there is nothing mystical or occult about what he is doing. Still, it is a rare wizard who can claim to be in his league when it comes to understanding and coercing others to do your bidding. As such, learning the same skills are essential and you could do a lot worse than to study Brown to see how he does it.

Harry Potter

And so we come to the most famous modern wizard of all, one who bears a lot of responsibility for the interest in spellcraft amongst the youth of today, Harry Potter. There can scarcely be a person on this planet who has not at least heard of young Harry with his lightning scar. Harry, of course, is a work of fiction, but his world bears more than a passing resemblance to that of the true wizard. There is little that Rowling writes about that is not found within the realms of wizardry. Herbalism, divination, numerology, familiars, etc., all form part of the modern wizard's training. Although it is dubious how far anyone could go if they decided to follow Potter's path into wizardry (it is, after all, fiction), the curriculum presented at Hogwarts is not far from what a real wizard should be expected to study.

So if we look at all these individuals collectively, we can get a pretty good idea of what makes a wizard. At the very least, you should be able to understand the nature of the elements and manipulate them according to need; summon and command spirits; have an army of familiars at your beck and call; learn the secret to allegedly impossible abilities, such as invisibility or immortality; traverse the astral; divine the future; understand not only the science but the art of magick; and have a strong understanding of the theory of magick, as well as experience of its practical application.

One thing which does stand out as a recurrent theme is the fact that so many wizards have also been con-men. Sadly, this is one of the pitfalls of a wizardly life. When you know just how easy it is to take advantage of your fellow Man, it is very difficult to resist the temptation to take advantage of the poor things. When you are aware that this is a potential side effect of following this path, it is much easier to avoid; whether you choose to avoid it is another question entirely and one for the individual to decide upon.

Paraphernalia - The Tools of Wizardry

We all know the (not so) stereotypical image of the witch huddled over her cauldron, wide-brimmed, black hat on head, broom in the corner, cackling away as she stirs up her potions and lotions, and whilst we are enlightened enough to know that this is more propaganda than any reflection of reality, still, witches do find use for cauldrons and broomsticks and herbal concoctions and although witches may more often be beautiful rather than haggard or buxom rather than skeletal, the stereotype has developed as a direct consequence of the truth. So what about us? What tools, if any, are required by the discerning wizard?

As with the witch, the widely held concept of what a wizard should look like and what tools he owns has a certain amount of basis in fact, although it is important to know where the line is between the exaggerated mass perception and the reality. Perhaps first we should ask, what do we think of when we think of a wizard? We imagine a man (usually), wearing a long robe and tall hat, grimoire in one hand, wand in the other, as he recites incantations in his room at the top of a tall tower. Taken straight out of a fantasy novel do you think? It might surprise you to learn that this is, in fact, a relatively accurate description and to demonstrate how fact based this image is, it would perhaps be helpful to take each item at a time and examine how and why it made its way into the toolkit of the wizard.

Robes and Hat

From antiquity we have accounts of ritual dress used only for specific ritual purposes. The wizard's robes and hat are therefore forming part of an ancient tradition which can be traced back for centuries and a mark of the respect and high esteem that we hold our Work in that we feel the need to dress up specially in honour of the ritual.

There are a number of reasons why it is important to have a set of clothing specifically set aside for your magickal practise. When we don our robes, we know that we are entering into magickal space, that we are about to embark upon an Otherworldly journey, deliberately leaving the mundane behind, so the changing of our clothes into our robe is part of the magickal ritual and a crucial part of the magickal preparation. Thus it is true that wizards do indeed have a *"uniform"* of sorts. However, there is no set pattern for what form this might take. We have our magickal clothing more to benefit the mind than the body, so you could, if you chose, wear a designer suit or even ripped jeans and T shirt for your magick just as easily as you could a robe, as long as it is something which is reserved solely for ritual purposes. However, wearing something which is akin to your everyday wear has less of an impact on the psyche when it comes to the concept of doing something outside of the norm. Not many people go about their daily lives wearing floor length heavy robes with esoteric patterns drawn about them (and for those who do, the ripped jeans option might be a better idea!).

Wizard's robes are frequently portrayed as purple with intricate yellow embroidery. The choice of purple with its flash opposite holds many significance, not least of which are the associations with Air, the element of the Mind and Intellect, which rule all wizardly endeavours, but it is the pattern which is of more interest, since each set of robes is unique to the individual. Not only do your robes mark a change in perception, they also have built into them one layer of your psychic armour and it is also for this reason that they would traditionally be made of silk, the material which confers the greatest protection against astral parasites. No arbitrary moon and star patterns for you when you perform your wizardry – leave romantic flim-flam to the wiclets; your robe and hat should be decorated with specific sigils, angelic or god names and warding symbols, all of which offer an extra layer of protection above and beyond anything that you work into your ritual, easing the pressure on you to ensure that you are guarded every step of the way.

Sigil :"Bugger off nasties"
by Aleq Grai

Even a silly, simple phrase like *"Bugger off nasties!"* can be reduced through atavistic sigilisation to a design which can be quite beautiful and artistic in its execution and makes the point very clearly to anything which would be foolish enough to mess with you. This is particularly important when dealing with unruly spirits for obvious reasons and on such occasions you may wish to create an extra item of clothing bespoke to the individual entity, either using symbols specifically associated with the being in question, such as those listed in the Goetia and other grimoires, or through further self designed sigilisation.

The hat serves a very similar function to the robes. It is not for nothing that a cap is frequently listed as being essential for magick of varying types and in covering our head, we ensure that all our chakras are covered (since the robe should also have a high neck, covering our throat chakra), except our third eye, allowing the focus to rest on our psychic vision.

Without the appropriate ritual clothing, it is impossible to be serious about your wizardry. If you do not respect your Work enough to ensure that you dress for the occasion, you will find that you will never achieve the results you desire. Have the courage to announce to the Universe that you truly intend to conquer its secrets and prove your resolve by putting the time, effort and money into creating the perfect uniform for yourself, one which will only ever be worn to Work. Over time your robes will almost feel like they take on a life of their own and you only have to put them on to be in magickal space already.

The Grimoire

Many self-professed solitary neo-pagans will announce with pride that their *"religion"* is not one of the book. How foolish. How can you go far unless you have stood on the shoulders of giants to view the horizon you wish to reach? As such, wizards feel no shame in admitting that there is worth to be found in following a trodden path until such a time as you reach uncharted land. There is so much forgotten knowledge lurking in the ancient texts waiting to be rediscovered. This is why it does this old wizard's heart good to see many of the medieval tomes being reprinted for a new generation of wizards and magickians to discover their mysteries without having to trawl the hidden depths of the British Library to find that missing piece of the puzzle.

Never underestimate the value of going back to basics and looking to those who have done the Work before you for inspiration. As anyone who has done any amount of practical magick can tell you, there is a world of difference between reading about something and experiencing it. It would be like reading a book describing what it is like to go swimming in the sea and thinking that you can therefore know just as much about it as someone who goes scuba diving on a regular basis, even though the closest you've ever been to the sea is your local fish and chip shop in Tring. There is great value to be had in recreating the work done by others to find more quickly what will be successful, what won't and what deliberate blinds have been placed to trip up the unwary.

Now you might eye the *Lemegeton* and think that there is an awful lot of material to be covered therein. And you would be right, but nevertheless, it must be done. Do not underestimate how much you need to do in order to truly describe yourself as following the Wizard's way. It is a rare person who is capable of creating their own grimoire from scratch and really, there is no need to reinvent the wheel when so many people have done such a good job before us. Having worked your way through the material provided to us by the likes of Agrippa, Dee, Rudd, Levi and Crowley, then perhaps you will be ready to put together your own contribution to the development and progress of human understanding and evolution and truly become a school of thought in your own right, the ultimate goal of any wizard, for, after all, how can you become immortal if you have not left your mark permanently on the world of magick?

The Magick Wand

Possibly the best known tool is the magick wand. Due to the proliferation of information distributed by the witches, who purloined this tool from the wizard in the first place, this probably needs the least explanation, but it is worth spending a moment addressing a few myths.

It is a lie that you should only pick for your wand a piece of wood which is already lying on the ground, having been discarded by the tree. Such wood is already dead and thus of no use to anyone. It is difficult to comprehend how anyone could imagine that it would have any ability to channel energy, yet somehow this myth has flourished and become embellished with all sorts of nonsense like needing to bury your '*wand*' after each use to return any negative energies to the earth... Sometimes, the mind boggles at what someone would be doing that such negativity would need to be earthed on such a regular basis.

Instead you need to go to the woods, announce your reason for being there to its inhabitants and walk through until you find a tree which doesn't just grant permission, but actively calls to you to take a piece of it. You should not find this difficult to hear and if in any doubt, simply placing your hand on the branch in question and asking whether it is acceptable for you to harvest a piece will instantly provide you with the answer you need. If you are mistaken in who you thought was calling to you, the tree will make its wishes very clear to you.

It is important that you be the one to harvest your wood and then craft your wand, for it will be used to focus your Will. No true wizard would waste his money paying someone else for a twig that could have come from anywhere with no guarantees of efficacy. Not for nothing is a wizard always pictured alone, with the possible exception of his familiar (a subject which is addressed in a separate chapter). We work by ourselves, for ourselves and this includes the crafting of our tools. Since they are so few anyway, this is hardly onerous and having found your wand, once you have treated it, cut it to the appropriate length (from elbow to fingertip), carved and decorated it, you will find yourself with an instrument which will serve you well for many, many years.

The Tower

The wizard's tower, so significant that it even holds a place in the witch's tarot deck, is perhaps the most mysterious and misunderstood item associated with wizardry. All too often it is assumed that the tower must be a real place, a building constructed on behalf of the wizard, far away from the cares of the world where he can hole himself up in its lofty heights and practise his magick far from the distractions of the world where he can do no harm to anyone but himself.

However, as with anything magickal, a solely literal interpretation gives a very distorted version of the truth. Your tower need not be a freestanding building. It can just as easily be your bedroom, study, back garden, or even (and here is where the biggest secret of all can be found) may not exist in reality at all. Your tower is so much more than a place; it is a state of mind. Your tower is reflected in your standing in the world. The greater your reputation and standing within your community, the greater your tower, which is why wizards are to be found wherever there is success. Anyone that claims to be leading a magickal life but lives in a permanent state of disaster has very little real understanding or experience of magick. Ever wondered why so many supposed witches and magickians lead such sad and sorry lives, lurching from one miserable failure to another? It's because they haven't yet realised that the magick works or, more importantly, that magick requires work. And it is that final key that unlocks your tower to you. The self discipline and work which is vital to a mastery of the wizard's way has a knock on effect. It is impossible to be a true master of your magick and not have this extend to other aspects of your life. If you have developed your intellect, powers of reasoning, memory, focus, concentration, etc., etc., in order to better practise your rituals, this simply cannot be kept in a little box and only taken out when you are being *"magickal"*. Those abilities will be brought to bear every day and allow you to perform even the most mundane of tasks with the maximum of effectiveness.

This is why it is a misconception that wizards live in tall towers. We do not live in our tower; we are our tower.

Familiar Companionship

The subject of familiars is one which frequently crops up on pagan discussion boards and the ensuing conversation usually goes something along these lines:

"Does anyone here have a familiar? My cat loves being around me whenever I do a ritual. I sometimes have to throw her off my lap so that I can meditate!"

"LOL! I know exactly what you mean. I have a black and white cat called Suki and a beautiful fluffy cat called Tina that I rescued as kittens. They are both my dearest friends and they are with me whenever I cast spells or talk to the Goddess(TM)"

"I did have a familiar. He was a Persian cat and really affectionate but he got run over a year ago. I still miss him very much."

And so follows a number of stories about feline friends, each going one step further than the last in tales of how adorable their little bundle of fur is and how much they love incense and candles, all of which do nothing but prove that few people have any real understanding of what having a familiar truly means and what their actual role should be. In these supposed enlightened times, going by such misguided stories, it appears that the only requirement a familiar needs to fulfil is the ability to pay attention to its backside while you light a candle and chant. Attractiveness is an optional extra.

If you are not serious about your magickal work, perhaps companionship and adoration is all you need, but if you are intent on plumbing the hidden depths of the universe, a more active participant is necessary, one who will be able to travel great distances for you, hunt and gather information and perform great acts behind the scenes on your behalf in order to achieve your Will. If you believe your pet is also your familiar, ask yourself this – when was the last time your animal gave you practical information which helped improve the efficacy of your magick? If the answer to this is never, I not so humbly suggest that you either content yourself with a mere pet, which is realistically all you have, or you take action to train your furry friend in the ways of magick so that they can sit by your side in true familial fashion.

So what form should a familiar take? Most people think of familiars as being cats, but in truth, these creatures are rarely suited to the role. If you own a cat, you own nothing more than the right to pay for its food and shelter, plus any medical attention that it may require. Any further "rights" are down to the cat's discretion, which goes where and when it will, while feeling under no obligation whatsoever to assist its master unless it be by catching the odd mouse. Should it so desire, a cat feels no compunction about moving in with the couple down the road who have a much comfier bed and provide it with steak every Sunday. Do not kid yourself. A cat chooses the human, not the other way round.

The wizard, of course, being wise, knows that it should always be he who is in the driving seat and thus goes for the infinitely superior route of the faithful hound, who is never happier than when performing useful tasks for its master and indeed, derives huge satisfaction from learning new things every day (one of the biggest secrets hidden in plain view is the myth that you can't teach an old dog new tricks. Not only is this not true, the older a dog gets, the deeper his magickal understanding becomes and the better he is at assisting you in the furtherance of your research). Who hasn't heard of Cornelius Agrippa and his black dog? The only mistake Agrippa made was to keep his dog so conspicuously by his side that it attracted suspicion, but then when your dog knows as much as his did, you wouldn't want it to fall into the wrong hands.

The traditional image of the guard dog takes on a whole new meaning when you consider that the dog would stand guard at the bounds of the magickal working, ensuring that no undesirable influence was able to enter and disturb the wizard. One of the biggest differences between a dog and a cat when it comes to their appropriateness as a familiar is that whilst they are both able to see Otherworldly entities, a cat will avoid any and every spirit at all costs, regardless of intention, whereas a dog will not only be able to tell the difference between the benevolent and malevolent, they will make sure that you are protected from any nasties, who will be reluctant to approach your Tower while your mutt is around. Since they are sensitive to the spirit world, they can sense the presence of any parasites and see them off without distracting the wizard, enabling him to pay full attention to his spells without having to waste any energy erecting wards. This is particularly useful when commanding spirits, since the tricky beasties will use anything they can to upset the wizard's concentration at delicate moments in an attempt to break free of their confines.

Dogs are also happy to lend any other support needed, allowing the wizard to draw upon their energy to provide a boost to his power if necessary, which can also be turned in the opposite direction and used as a grounding mechanism. And of course we should not forget the role of spy, since few people bother to pay any attention to minding their behaviour in front of the dog, allowing the wizard to obtain a fuller picture of those who would work with him without their knowing.

Of course, what neo-pagans have mainly failed to understand is the fact that a physical entity is only half of the picture and that no true wizard would ever be without his spirit familiars. Even if you never own an animal in your life, you will not want to be without your Otherworldly familiars.

As you progress further down the path of wizardry, you will find that you naturally attract all sorts of astral entities. Some will be benign, some not so much and others downright evil. As such, it is important to perform regular reviews of the spirits within your Tower to ensure that only those that are serving your interests are around you. However, should you discover that you have accumulated some of the less savoury entities, this is not necessarily a bad thing, since you will, in the course of mastering the art of commanding spirits, learn techniques which allow you to bind them to your Will, should you so choose, swelling the ranks of your minions – and a wizard can never have too many minions. Alternatively, you can offer them the chance to return to their natural habitation and should they refuse to leave, render them into a karmic zero. This is one of the most satisfying experiences, since any parasite which is so intent on remaining around solely to cause trouble serves no useful function and not only are you squashing one of the most malicious bugs you can encounter, you are doing the universe a favour by removing them from the food chain.

However, you should not rely solely on your personal attractiveness to build your ranks of familiars. It is important that you actively seek to swell your support network and one extremely valuable source of this are the ancient grimoires, such as the *Goetia*. Many of the beings listed in there are cited as "*granting good familiars*" and having legions of spirits at their command. Obviously you will want to exercise care in who you choose to perform this service for you, since not only are the Goetic entities of varying levels of usefulness, some being easier to order than others, but so are the spirits at their command and you will want to ensure that you have ones working for you which are compatible with the work you are doing. You would do well to learn the subtleties and nuances of each specific word used in the description of the demons, since a variation of even one alters the sphere of influence of the entity and their legions. You could, for example, obtain for yourself familiars of the Order of Thrones or the Order of Virtue, and I'm sure you don't need me to explain to you just how helpful it could be to have angelic beings working on your behalf.

So why would you want a familiar you can't see, a spirit being who is of no use when it comes to keeping your toes warm when it sleeps at the foot of your bed at night or who cannot sit on your lap and snuggle when you are feeling down? The answer is blindingly obvious to any true wizard. These things are fleeting, and are of little value when it comes to a Higher Purpose. A spirit familiar might not be able to nuzzle you, but that moment of eureka in the middle of the night when you suddenly obtain the hidden key to that difficult magickal conundrum you'd been pondering? Familiar. That piece of inspiration when you're searching for exactly the right words to perfect the ritual you are crafting? Familiar. That chance meeting with that certain someone who turned out to be able to teach you that technique you needed to master or provide you with a tool that you were in desperate need of? Familiar.

If you have an open, reciprocal working relationship with your spirit familiars, you will find that the more work they do for you, the easier things become, to the point where you will never even need to worry about finding a parking space again, because they will have gone on ahead to have cleared the way so that even at the busiest of times, you find yourself able to park right in front of that shop you needed to visit to top up your wizardry supplies. After all, if you are wasting time having to drive round looking for a space and then trekking all the way back to where you want to go, that's time that you are unable to spend on your magickal work. It's a familiar's very duty to ensure that you are free to study and practise your magick as much as you need.

As a wizard, which type of familiar do you think is the most useful?

Pointing and Laughing

Let me begin with a story. A story of witchcraft. It is a true story and tells of one of the best examples of cursing I have encountered. Are you sitting comfortably?

Our tale concerns a woman. A witch, to be more exact, and one who was extremely circumspect about her business, being more than happy to perfect her Craft quietly, in the shadows. Yet, despite her best efforts, word got out as to what she was and some fishwives took it upon themselves to make her life most uncomfortable. When the opportunity came to move far, far away, the witch was very relieved indeed to be leaving them behind, although not without giving the ringleader a parting gift.

By the light of the full moon, she took a piece from one of the herbs in her garden, planted it in a pretty pot and gave it to her former friend, telling her *"Traditionally rosemary is grown to ward against witchcraft. I have two plants in my garden, one in the front and one in the back. This cutting is harvested from them and given to you to pay you back for everything you've done for me. Look after it and it will look after you."* So saying, she walked away and never looked back. The witch had her revenge in spades, for the woman was in a quandary. Take the plant into her house and care for it and she might be nurturing a curse; let it die and she might be allowing evil spirits to be released and so it made no difference whether the cutting survived or not – from that moment on, anything bad that happened was automatically the result of the curse placed on the plant whilst the witch had the perfect alibi, living hundreds of miles away. A curse that existed nowhere but in the recipient's mind.

One cannot help but admire the artistry that went into that piece of non-magick. However, the purpose of sharing this tale is not to praise the witch's way, but to demonstrate how so much of what they do is nothing but playing on the fears of the superstitious, but in the sneakiest, most underhand way possible. Mere psychology, dressed up in a witch's hat with a wart on the nose. It is genius, requires great skill and talent, but it is not magick.

This spotlights one of the biggest difference between witches and wizards. We do not hide anything that we do. We do not lurk in the shadows – we declare our intentions openly and with integrity. Which means that if someone is being foolish, we point and laugh and have absolutely no compunction in taking advantage of the fact. If someone wishes to be an idiot, let them. It makes our task all the easier. Whilst the witch's curse was beautifully crafted, it was a waste of effort and energy, time that could have been better spent elsewhere.

A wizard would have simply walked away without a backward glance, knowing that someone as unenlightened and ignorant as that is not only unworthy of your attention, but that there is nothing you can do to them that is any worse than the living hell they keep themselves in day by day of their own making, as they live trapped within the confines of the limits they place upon themselves.

Attitude is all. A witch spends her time working for others; a wizard works solely for himself. How selfish! I hear you gasp. But in fact, nothing could be further from the truth. A wizard knows that it is impossible to be of any good to anyone unless you have your own house in order first. Think of your relationship with your Craft as being like any marriage. You are in no position to make your partner happy unless you are happy yourself. Sacrificing yourself on the altar of your beloved and allowing them to trample all over you not only earns you disdain rather than respect, it leaves you both miserable. No matter how hard you try to satisfy someone else, if you are not first pleased, all your efforts will be for nothing.

And so it is in wizardry. If you are not constantly striving to push your boundaries, to go as far as you can possibly go, to be the best you can possibly be, you are no wizard. Only when you have reached that pinnacle can you reach down to help others up to your level. And help them you must, for the onus on wizardry is the evolution of mankind and sometimes that evolution can be tough for only the fittest will survive.

Frittering time away on internet forums is a distraction, but if you can limit yourself it can, on occasion, prove a useful lesson in not only demonstrating just how idiotic people can be when they really put their mind to it, but also allow you to hone your intellect and skills of reasoning and you may even, if you are very lucky, be the lighthouse that allows the favoured few to find the way. It can be an amusing diversion to remind yourself just how stupid some idiots can be and how easy it is to fall into the trap of thinking that you know more than you actually do.

But be careful – shooting fish in a barrel will only do so much to improve your hunting skills, so whilst it is so, so easy to get suckered in to arguing with those who won't get it, no matter how much you explain, you are better off setting your sights higher, finding worthy opponents who have just as much to offer you as you do to them. Otherwise, you are simply wasting time trying to help those who neither deserve nor will use your help. And it is always worth making a head count of how many complain of how they have no time for the Work, or who are looking for a quick shortcut to the same result because they would like the experience but say that they are unable to follow the usual path, yet are capable of posting countless, pointless messages on the Net. A wizard knows that he who shouts loudest for longest is invariably blowing hot air.

Trickery

Anyone who has read the chapter on the men and myths of wizardry will have noticed a recurrent theme. Many, many wizards have been accused of fraud, forgery or downright con-artistry (and these accusations have not exactly been without water). It is not surprising; as WC Fields put it, it's morally wrong to allow a sucker to keep his money and when you realise just how simple it is to take advantage of the general stupidity of your fellow man, it is all too easy to do it, just because you can. Now I make no moral judgement here about whether this is a good thing or not – that is for the individual to decide – but should you be inclined to follow that sort of path, to begin with, I recommend you check out *Mind Magic* by Marc Lemezma for many easy-to-master examples of ways in which you can quickly establish yourself as someone with genuine mystical powers, if that is what you wish to do.

However, before you embark upon this route, consider the long term consequences of setting yourself up as something you are not. It does not matter how many times Derren Brown (or any other stage magician) states that he has no psychic powers, there will always be those who claim to know what he is doing better than he does and since they believe they are psychic and that this is the only mechanism to achieve the results he does (in their opinion), therefore, he must be lying about his abilities – either that, or actually be a latent psychic but unaware of his innate talents. Of course, he is telling the truth and to my mind, what he does is far more skilful than mere mind reading, but still, you need to think through the impact on your day to day life of convincing your friends and acquaintances that you are in possession of occult abilities. It was not so long ago that families were torn apart under accusations of satanic abuse and whilst it is now recognised that this was and is a myth, the mindset that gave rise to children being taken away because of fear of the unknown is still very much alive and well in our culture. It may not be illegal to be clairvoyant or a mystic, but that won't stop the ignorant or superstitious causing problems for you if they believe you to be a danger to society. Once you have convinced someone of your psychic abilities, it is virtually impossible to disabuse them of that fact, even if you tell them exactly how you managed to trick them in the first place, and there are those who believe that actively living a lie will have long term consequences not only on your mental well being but also on your physical health.

Scaring the natives aside, there is more to the art of trickery than meets the eye – and you can have a lot more fun by exploring its full potential instead of wasting your energies kidding other people. Words have a greater meaning and more power than most people realise. It is all too often assumed that magickal writing should be taken literally and only literally, and when you consider how fantastical some of the abilities ascribed to wizards (and indeed, witches) are, you could be forgiven for assuming that these descriptions are exaggeration or even downright lies. However, such an interpretation misses the subtleties and nuances of language that magick employs to such wonderfully great effect.

Take, for example, the question of immortality. It is all too easy to assume that this automatically means eternal life, but in fact, the dictionary gives us no less than three definitions: eternal life; life after death; and enduring fame. As such, it should immediately become apparent that there are a number of ways one can achieve this. One is to simply reproduce. Have children, the more the merrier, and see that they in turn continue the line, thus ensuring that your genetic code survives down through the generations, carrying a little piece of you with it. Another is to leave your mark on the world. Write a classic bestseller, become a film star in a popular movie, perform a groundbreaking piece of scientific research, win a Nobel Prize. None of these are particularly easy to achieve for the average person – but then, a wizard is hardly average and nobody said that immortality was easy, just that it is possible. And of course, there is always the option of the Great Work.

So there you have it. The secret of immortality in a paragraph, no Philosopher's Stone required.

So what of other wizard's tricks? Does this mean that everything a wizard is alleged to be capable of is possible? Absolutely. Nothing is impossible if you truly put your mind to it. Want to become invisible? You can have that one mastered before lunchtime and what's more, you don't even have to work hard at something deeply arcane like changing your aura or projecting your Will into someone else's mind. And here's how.

Again, we need to consider what the word actually means. Most people's first assumption is that turning invisible meanings somehow becoming see-through, much like the Invisible Man of so many books and films or Harry Potter's Cloak of Invisibility, so that you can be standing right in front of someone and they don't see you. Leaving aside the fact that this is, indeed, possible, to be invisible can also denote being out of sight or hidden; not perceptible or discernible by the mind; concealed from public view. I'm sure that once you consider the alternative interpretations of the word you can already begin to see how wizards can most definitely be invisible. The simple fact of not telling anyone of your magickal work automatically confers invisibility, since you have hidden from the general public what exactly you are. If no one knows you have a secret, then that secret is truly hidden and you can stand right in front of anyone and no matter how hard they might be searching for a true wizard, they will not know you are there.

Can you see me?

A Demonstration of the Art of Invisibility

Consider how many other ways there are to hide in plain sight. The internet, for example, makes it shockingly easy to track down old flames and acquaintances. How many of us have Googled the name of a lost friend at one time or another? It is quite frightening how much information people will post about themselves, full name, photographs of themselves and their families, details of themselves and their loved ones, their past, current and future plans, etc., etc. So think about how you can stand unseen amongst such information overload – don't use your real name or change your date of birth for each and every service you sign up to; choose a name which is common so that someone looking for you won't know which John Smith is actually you; keep personal information to a minimum so that it is difficult or impossible to work out who you are by inference; be wary of even providing clues as to where you live.

Such caution may seem excessive to those used to these times of blogs and *LiveJournals* where people write about their lives for all to see without a care for who may be looking, but it is not for nothing that many of these people are now choosing to hide their entries from all but a select few, having learnt the hard way the folly of being so high profile. As a wizard, it is likely that you will be beleaguered by those wanting you to perform a service for them or even those wishing you harm purely because you choose to follow a magickal path; you may well find that it serves you well in the long term to become invisible right from the start.

Let us assume, for the moment, that you were to take the path of the con artist. If you were to live a life of lies, to do so successfully, you need to believe every lie you tell, even if it's only for that moment. But more, you need to move past believing to a state of knowing. It is not for nothing that the maxim of the Magus contains *"To Know"* and why it is said that magick has no room for belief. For something to work, it is not enough to merely believe that if you think you are invisible, you will be. You have to Know, with every essence of your being that you are invisible. Someone who considers themselves to be a wall flower will inevitably be viewed as such by those around them. Many adolescents go through this phase until they develop a stronger sense of self awareness and confidence. If you were one of them, try to think back and remember how that felt, how you felt, the kind of thoughts and feelings that ran through your mind during this period and regain that sense of worthlessness.

Question with every fibre of your being, why on earth would anyone bother to notice you when you are so beneath them? Immersing yourself in your new role, go to any crowded bar and attempt to order yourself a drink. I guarantee you that you will be passed over in favour of the more vocal and assertive time and time again until someone finally gets round to bothering with you. Once more, you can be standing right in front of someone and they completely fail to notice you. Now, you might think that this is a rather useless skill and when it comes to quenching your thirst, I agree. But consider how much more useful this might be if you want people to talk on a subject without considering whether you can hear them or not. It would be extremely valuable indeed to be able to sit there and eavesdrop and know that you are doing no wrong because you are in plain view of the speakers at all times. Many a juicy, useful tidbit of information has been garnered using this technique.

I'm sure you don't need me to go on and on and on debunking and laying bare the inner core of each and every wizardly trick in the book. It should be more than obvious to the discerning reader that the hidden secret to each and every one of them is deceptively simple and easy to master should you care to take the time to figure out the key. This is one of the reasons why I personally choose to avoid the path of the fraud – a mere con is just too easy and offers no real challenge to a real wizard. It is much more interesting and personally rewarding to explore the techniques of wizardry and come up with creative methods and inventive uses to which to put them. Whilst the temptation of chicanery may lie in the illusion that it is a quick path to great wealth and standing, the reality is that once you are exposed (and the likelihood is that you will be eventually), all that hard work will have been for nothing.

A look at the life of Frank Abignale, a multi-millionaire and the inspiration behind the film *Catch Me If You Can*, is an abject lesson in the fact that whilst crime might pay, you need to be a genius at what you do in order to make it pay well and if you have that level of ability, it makes more sense to pour that energy into more legitimate practises that are equally profitable but do not carry the same level of risking personal liberty, all important to anyone doing the Great Work. Any wizard who has mastered his Craft will have found along the way that the skills he has honed will have flowed over into other aspects of his life. It is impossible to be a successful wizard and not also be a success at everything else you do.

The *James Randi Education Foundation* has put up $1,000,000 as a prize for anyone who is able to successfully demonstrate paranormal abilities. To this date, no one has won, despite the plethora of psychics, mediums, witches, druids, shamans, spirit healers, etc., that populate the globe. To the casual observer, this provides more than enough proof that magick is a lie the gullible tell themselves every day. And it is a good question – for those who truly believe themselves to be an actual practitioner of the Occult, and reliably so, why has no one been able to claim it? Personally I believe there are many reasons for this, not least of which the fact that those who have mastered invisibility rarely have the wish to undo all that hard work by exposing themselves to the world as someone who can successfully demonstrate supernatural phenomena.

Quite simply, there are far too many scared people who would react badly to such news. However, another factor is the simple reality is that magick is, at the heart of it, mundane. It concerns itself more with the spiritual than the material, it is a way of life and, moreover, it is a way with words. If you were to present yourself to the JREF as someone who is able to turn invisible at will and demonstrated this by your inability to be served in a bar, you might provide them with a moment's hilarity, but although you have technically demonstrated that you are telling the truth, since anybody can do this, you are hardly proving yourself to be otherworldly.

This is why so many people are so disappointed when they discover the truth about magick and why the books which promise grand returns and weave beautiful fantasies sell so well – it is not for nothing that magick is described as both an art and a science. It works. It provides demonstrable, repeatable results that anyone can experience should they choose to take the time to learn how. So much of it is all in the mind; it is how you choose to view the world. This is not to say that wizardry is all trickery and playing with words, but it certainly forms the inner core of much of its workings. This may well be disappointing to those who would prefer to live in a dream world, but this is to deny the richness that magick can bring to your day to day living if you can shift your perceptions to encompass it.

If you are finding it disheartening to be told that the secret to most magickal skills is in the interpretation, move past this and rather than focus on the fact that your dream of waltzing down the high street naked with no one knowing has just gone up in smoke, consider how much more useful the reality of invisibility actually is. Most people are drawn to wizardry because they want quick and easy results and they believe that magick promises this. Nothing worth having is ever handed to you on a plate. It's all in the presentation.

The Art & Science of Divination

It seems almost otiose to state that being able to see into the future is a very important skill indeed. It doesn't take a huge leap of imagination to realise that if you could truly know what will happen with absolute certainty, there is an enormous amount of power that confers. Forget trying to influence the Wheel of Fortune with the power of your mind – you are struggling against all those other thousands of would-be winners willing their numbers to turn up. How much easier it would be if you could simply divine the numbers which will be drawn. You too could win the National Lottery!

Everyone has some latent psychic ability to one degree or another. Anyone who is willing to put in the effort to hone their skills will find themselves improving with each attempt. The more you listen to that inner voice, the more you discover how uncannily accurate and truthful it is. This is not your spirit guide speaking to you or your guardian angel or those who have passed before or anything else others might tell you are dealing with. We wizards do not, as a rule, defer to others to tell us what we need to know (the only exception being when commanding spirits, a separate issue and one with a chapter devoted to it). We know that we are born with everything we need and that we have no use for handing over responsibility to an otherworldly entity or trusting *"spirit"* to tell us what to do. A good wizard chooses his method and his tools wisely and knows that there is as much a scientific approach to foretelling as there is the art of interpretation.

The Question of *the Question*

Regardless of which technique you choose to perfect, you will still need to master the art of crafting the perfect query(ies). Your divination is only as good as the questions you ask. Garbage in, garbage out. Think of that wonderful old wives' tale, that dangling a wedding ring in front of a woman's pregnant belly will tell you the gender of the child therein. Using a pendulum is a common low magick technique, but notoriously unreliable, especially if you do not tailor your questions to be as specific as possible. In the early days of pregnancy, asking the gender of your child will invariably bring the reply *"female"*, whereas waiting a few weeks may well bring a different answer. Why? Because every fetus starts off as female! A minor alteration to the question so that it becomes *"what will be the gender of this child when it is born"* will give you a much more dependable response. See how important it is to make sure your question is well crafted and appropriate?

At its basic root, divination is nothing more than being able to see the patterns of the universe, whether you view it as wyrd, fate, a tapestry, whatever, and know where they are leading. If you continue on the path you currently are, you will arrive at a particular destination, so if you do not like where you are heading, make a conscious decision to take a different fork now. Simple methods have their time and place. However, a wizard, such as you hope to be, is not interested in vagaries. You want your information to be as specific as possible. As such, the more primitive techniques are of little or no use to you. As can be seen by the example above, if you are limited to asking questions that can only be answered with yes or no, you need to be highly skilled in the manner in which you craft your questions and even then, when you think that you have covered every eventuality, if there is a factor which you are unaware of or have not considered, you could still end up with results which are next to worthless.

As is so often the case with any kind of magick, precision is key and words have power. If you wish to know whether a business venture will be successful, it is of no use to ask *"will this be successful?"* When in discussion with a human adviser, they will know what you mean and what you are hoping to hear, as well as the difference between that and what you need to hear. The world of fortune telling is never that straightforward. What do you mean by successful? Breaks even? Makes a profit? Brings you social status? Will it be easy? Within what time frame? What kind of hours will you need to put in to achieve this? Will it be something you enjoy? The English language has so many nuances, it is vital to make sure that you put together a set of questions which makes allowances for these and leaves no wriggle room whatsoever. Otherwise you may find yourself following advice which is totally appropriate and accurate within your frame of reference, but which, in hindsight turns out to be for a completely different scenario to the one which you'd envisaged. Approach your divining of future outcomes with as open a mind as to possible answers, do not ask any question you do not wish to know the answer to (it is little comfort to know the time and manner of your own death, for example), but do not open up your mind so much your brains slither out.

Consulting the Dead

So what methods of divination should a wizard devote his attentions to? In ancient times, no wizard was truly worthy of the title until he had demonstrated competency in *extispicy*, otherwise known as the reading of entrails. Such a practice would be abhorrent to modern day diviners and rightly so – there is no need for it when there are other methods which return equal or better results and don't involve animal rights activists banging on your door. Nevertheless, in the past, when ritual sacrifice ensured a reliable supply of reading matter to experiment with, it was a relatively easy task to learn the signs and symbols that could reveal all about the times to come. Why it was that entrails could prove to be this useful, is not entirely clear. Given the proliferation of mediums and those who consult the spirits via ouija boards and such like, it is clear that necromancy still has a tight grip over us today and since the point of death is the most powerful release of energy from any being, it is hardly surprising that reading the inner organs of a recently slaughtered beast will give uncanny insights into the inner secrets of the universe. As above, so below.

However, since any genuine seeker would feel no need to sully their hands with the blood of innocents, so the modern day wizard should turn his attentions elsewhere. If you wish to remain true to the spirit of extispicy (if you'll pardon the pun), a method which is more socially acceptable in these enlightened times is osteomancy or divination with bones. The Sunday roast wishbone takes on a whole new meaning when you consider how the crude superstition of pulling the bone to make a wish can be turned to more serious matters by asking your question as you tug at it. Should you be successful, the answer obviously is yes; should you fail, the reply is in the negative. Effective as a basic introduction to the concept of omens, but highly limited since you can only ask questions that require a yes/no response and then only as many questions as you have bones (and unless you live in an unusually large family, the chances are, you'll have one bone, so need to be absolutely certain you are asking the right thing).

Alternatively, you can craft your own set of bones to read. Only the foolhardy or showy would even bother considering working with human bones, likewise, any creature who relies on scavenging for its food is not a suitable candidate for your set, but if you can acquire bones from a reliable, humane source, not only will you appease those who would use any excuse to persecute the wizard, you will have a tool which will help you throughout the entirety of your magickal career. Even better if you can find bones that are associated with an animal you have an affinity with, whether this be an alleged totem animal or actual companion – a former familial servant can prove faithful even from beyond the grave and wizards are nothing if not thrifty and practical.

Once you have your bones, you have a choice in how you use them. Either you can assign a specific meaning to each individual bone and treat them much as you might runes, spontaneously selecting an appropriate number to answer a particular question or you can cast them and read the patterns that form where they lie. You might wish to craft a casting cloth with specific signs and sigils on it to assist in this process, bones falling outside of the circle being of no consequence, for example. Since each set of bones is so unique, it really is up to the individual wizard to develop his own method of working.

Your Future In Stars

For those to whom dealing with the dead is anathema, there are other methods which are of equal antiquity and have centuries of study and honing behind them to create systems beautiful in their intricacy. You could do worse for a starting point than the noble art of astrology, which pays dividends in more ways than one. If a wizard has an in-depth knowledge of the secrets of the stars, not only does he gain a deep understanding of the tides ruling events on the earth and where they will lead us, but more than that, he enriches his appreciation of correspondences, their pattern and correlation and why it is that certain combinations such as a mutable earth sign or a fixed water sign will hold the influence that they do. This hold on the power of association will naturally inform his other work and enable him to craft his magick almost instinctively, as the influences of the planets, sun and moon is felt more deeply and noticeably than by the uneducated. The phase of the moon and the zodiac house it is currently occupying, the time of day, even the time of year, all can be used to ensure your magick achieves optimum results and the more you immerse yourself in them, the closer you will come to a state of being where you no longer need to consult charts to know what phase the moon is in or whether Mercury is retrograde – you will be able to feel it in the air and observe its effects in those around you.

One of the advantages that astrology holds over other types of divination is that it falls more into the category of science in that the chart says what it says. There is no issue of asking spirit for assistance or misinterpreting what your gut instinct is telling you. Either the planets are favourable or they are not. Although there is a certain degree of individual variance, just as different students can study the same text for an exam and draw differing conclusions as to the motives of the characters therein, the basic tides will remain the same regardless of who is studying them.

Should you decide that astrology is not for you, I still highly recommend any wizard obtain at least a basic working knowledge of it. It does not take a great leap of faith to understand that a spell cast at a time when the moon and sun are in appropriate astrological houses will have a greater chance of success than one which is performed without any care for the flow of the universe. In addition, an appreciation of the attributes associated with each sign, their element, the impact on the planets, etc., will assist greatly in building your knowledge of correspondences and how they all fit together. It bears repeating; as above, so below.

The Four Elements

Since the four elements form the basis of any magickal system, any wizard worth his salt will find the art of scrying pitifully easy to master. However, do not dismiss its power purely because it is simple to do. The elements may be playful and capricious when the whim takes them, but they are bound to the truth. If you know how to access their inner depths, their wisdom will astound you and unlike systems where you are constricted by yes/no questions, once you have engaged the attention of an element, you should be able to enter into an in-depth dialogue with it and explore all the possible options and outcomes until you know without doubt what is the best course of action open to you.

Although it is worth having some experience with each of the elements, when you speak to one, you speak to all and it is not necessary to attain the same level of skill in scrying with each. Experiment with them all, then focus on the one which you have found most responsive to your call. You may be surprised as to which one that is. The most commonly chosen is fire and indeed, many a lay person has spent hours gazing into the flame, watching the patterns and pictures dancing therein, mesmerised by the scenes unfolding, followed by water, where staring at your reflection into a darkened pool has a certain narcissistic charm, resulting in a trance state to enable you to see beyond yourself. Reading the smoke from burning incense can yield good results, but whilst the image of the gypsy woman with her crystal ball is a pervasive myth and the one which most think of when discussing scrying, few wizards bother with such a cliché.

Which method you choose is up to you, but you may well find that, if you have followed my suggestion to obtain a basic command of astrology, once you have cast your birth chart, you are dominant in one particular element, and it is this element which will be the most loquacious when you consult it. Conversely, should there be one which is noticeably lacking in your chart, you may well find that this is the one you struggle with. Having stated that it is best to work with the element you find easiest, since this will most quickly produce results, as a matter of discipline, you should aim to hone your skills with the hardest when you have the opportunity in order to balance out your abilities and strengthen your magick as a whole.

Consulting External Beings

If you have journeyed far down the path of wizardry, then you will be familiar with the practice of evocation. It does not take long before the call of the circle and triangle become too seductive to ignore. There are various beings who can tell you of the future, but this is not recommended as a reliable method, since spirits are notorious liars if you have not obtained 100% control and command over them, and whilst much of what they tell you can be verified, when dealing with the future, the only way of knowing if they have been truthful is to wait and see! It is more than within the ability of a mischievous being to tell the truth about things you can check (such as past and current events) to lull you into a false sense of security and believe that it must therefore be telling the truth about the future as well. Any divination should be taken as a guide rather than set in stone and it would be all too easy to allow yourself to follow a spirit's advice and discover that you have been set up for a fall, by which point it is too late to correct your mistake. It is all very well and good to threaten a spirit with punishment if it is lying if you have made such a mess of your life that this is no longer possible. It does not take a genius to understand why this is not a particularly desirable scenario and this is why, as a general rule, wizards do not take other's words for what is to come – they see it for themselves.

However, there is one mechanism to circumvent this. If you have the means and ability, binding a spirit into a physical container, such as a ring or necklace constrains it and forces it to be truthful, since you have the power of life and death over it. Any misbehaviour or transgression is easily punished and the entity you have chosen knows this and therefore knows that it is bound to do as you will until such a time that you release it. Or sell it on eBay.

Astral Projection

"And 'tis an art well known to Wizards old
And wily Hags, who oft for fear and shame
Of the coarse halter, do themselves withold
From bodily assisting their night game.
Wherefore their carcasses do home retain,
But with their souls at these bad feasts they are,
And see their friends and call them by their name,
And dance about the Goat and sing har, har,
And kiss the Devil's breech, and taste his deadly cheer"

Henry More, 1647

This extract demonstrates a crucial point about astral projection, namely that it is a key technique, whether you are dealing with High Magick (like wizardry) or Low (like witchcraft). It is a huge subject, one fit for many volumes in itself, as evinced by the plethora of books out there covering it; however, as you might suspect, there is an awful lot of misinformation out there and, as is so often the way, wading through it all to find the truth lurking within can be an arduous task.

Astral projection, as its name would suggest, involves the projecting of the astral body out of the physical in order to explore the realms of the astral. According to magickal theory, the astral plane is connected to the physical, as it is to other realms, but runs at a higher level of vibration and thus is more readily accessed by our astral selves, which is also that part of us which survives the death of our bodies.

There are many uses for the astral, including divination (visitors to the Akashic record are able to access all knowledge of the universe, including all experience and understandings known to man. You will find that many will claim to have accessed them; how many have genuinely done so is for you to determine). Another is in the construction of thought forms, entities similar to familiars in that they are designed to further your Will, but different in that they are your own creation and thus subject entirely to whatever contract you deem appropriate (and I would strongly recommend you always include a termination date and a reminder that as an extension of your Will, they are subject to be obedient to you alone and not to involve themselves in any other business). There are also many astral beings, ranging from elementals through to discarnate human souls and even animal souls, which will be of varying use to you, some helpful and some downright malignant. The ability known as Second Sight can be attributed to seeing into the astral and noticing these creatures whilst still firmly based in the physical.

Many techniques have been proposed to assist the individual to project. One author suggests that if you simply wish for it hard enough, you will spontaneously burst from your body and into your astral, but alas, you can spend many, many hours doing this and develop nothing more than a crick in your neck as your body strains to escape itself through sheer will power alone. A more common method (and unsurprisingly, more successful) is to create a doppelganger of yourself floating above your body. Focus on visualising someone identical to you in every way, right down to the clothes you are wearing, the position you are lying in, the placement of every hair on your head. Then place your consciousness in your astral body and view the world from a few feet above your physical body. Look about you, see how things look differently from your new perspective. Then be brave and start to move about, exploring your immediate surroundings until you realise that you are no longer tied to your body and are free to roam wherever you desire. With practise and perseverance, you will find that you are able to access the astral planes whenever you choose, thus opening up for yourself an entirely new realm to experience and comprehend.

Astral projection is frequently confused with lucid dreaming, which, while it can be a precursor to astral work, is not entirely the same thing. Lucid dreaming is simply being aware that you are in the dream state and taking control of it as such. This technique, whilst being of use to the wizard in terms of exerting dominance over your subconscious, has a number of applications, again demonstrating that when you perfect magickal skills, they frequently have more use than the obvious. For example, if you suffer from recurrent nightmares, it is a small matter to take control of your dream and turn the tables on your tormentors. It is, after all, your mind, so it is your rules that should apply. Likewise, if you are nervous about an up and coming business presentation, you can take control of your dreams to practise the scenario that most concerns you so that when you are faced with it in the real world, you have conquered your fears and are able to deal with it brimming with confidence.

Keeping a dream diary is the most basic of magickal practises and one which should form part of your daily routine. Not only will this hone your recollections and assist you in controlling your mind in preparation to explore it, it will enable you to spot recurrent themes, which may contain a clue as to what is most important to you right now, as well as allowing you to keep your eyes open for any omens which may appear, helping you to develop your psychic powers of divination. Moreover, this is a quick and easy way of proving to yourself that daily practise works – if you are diligent in recording your dreams on a daily basis, you will find that it is only a matter of days, weeks at the utmost, before you are recalling a minimum of one vivid dream a night, if not more.

Once you are able to remember your dreams regularly, you will then be able to move onto working lucidly. Many techniques have been detailed which can assist this (and the bibliography contains further reading on the subject), including visualising a simple image before you go to sleep or performing 'dream checks' to see whether you are asleep or awake (where the custom of pinching yourself to see if you're dreaming originates). You will find that when you first become lucid, you shock yourself awake, but with perseverance, you will find yourself able to maintain it for longer and longer periods, and there are little tricks you can employ to aid you in remaining in this state, such as performing some kind of physical activity, focussing your mind on maintaining the illusion rather than realising you are actually lying in bed and once you are lucid, you are limited only by your imagination in what you do with that.

Herb Lore

At first glance, it would appear that herb lore has more to do with witchcraft than it does wizardry. After all, we all know of the image of the *"wise woman"* dispensing herbs for those in need of healing and for centuries, midwives have used herbs to ease labour and deal with the transition into the world of parenthood. However, a wizard would ignore the realms of plants at his peril and their uses extend far further than a simple heal or hurt.

A popular children's tale is *Sleeping Beauty*. As is the case with so many fairy stories, there are little hints as to the reality of magick and when you consider that the Beauty is held within a tower not unlike a wizard's, it should not take a huge leap of imagination to understand that the wall of thorns protecting it is one which can be found in real life. Now there is a hidden meaning to this (after all, what would a magickal text be if it couldn't be read on a number of levels) and it can be taken to referring the focussed Will against any comers, but even taken purely literally, it is not as unlikely a scenario as others you might find in fiction.

Thorny plants have often been used as a cheap (and legal) deterrent to anyone who might be tempted to climb over a wall to trespass. Sometimes magickal theories have their basis in very mundane reality. After all, a plant which demand blood payment on anyone attempting to get past will do much to put off those looking for a quick and easy entry and one which is cared for by the owner of its garden will be more than willing to repay the care and attention lavished upon it. Roses, for example, will not only entangle trespassers in their thorns, their flowers and the oils obtained from them can be used very effectively to bless the home. Barberry will trap evil spirits in its barbs, as will that sacred tree, the holly. However, there are other, more subtle, associations with plants that may be planted to ward off evil. Rosemary, for example, has been traditionally grown to fend off witches and it is not the only kitchen herb that can offer this service – sage is another that will stop an intruder in his tracks. Lilies planted along the path leading up to the home will cast a charm over it, protecting those who reside there. Many trees are said to confer protection against the home they cast their shadow over – rowans, apples and elders are particularly benevolent and many will talk of the friendliness they receive at the foot of an oak. However, be careful in your choices here – whilst cypress will do the same, it is traditionally a rather serious tree and can make what would otherwise be a happy home a rather sombre and depressive one, albeit one safe from attack.

The plants that you choose to grow in the garden of your Tower can all have a magickal association, strengthening not just the defences of your home but also empowering the wizard and improving those aspects of himself he wishes to emphasise. If we look at the physical ability of many herbs, this can be carried through to a magickal conclusion, e.g. Chamomile has cleansing properties and is a good drink for bedtime, since it relaxes the individual and encourages positive feelings. Grown in the garden, its presence is uplifting and attracts happy, supportive energies. Likewise, if a wizard makes their own incense (and most do, since it is a rare one who would risk anyone else's energies mingling with theirs), the power of that incense is increased greatly if the herbs used are able to be harvested from a source that you have personally nurtured and tended.

Another use of plants which is frequently overlooked is in the manufacturing of inks. They may be used to colour cloth and hide, write with, decorate the skin and hair and anything else that colours may be required to add a further dimension to your magick. A very simple way of doing this is to simply use the plant's sap as it comes, applied directly to stain a surface. Many colours may be obtained in this manner, from the basic green through to vivid reds and purples, not forgetting the blues associated with woad. The quality of ink obtained from plants is limited only by the wizard's ability to prepare them – water is most frequently used as a base, the correct part of the plant(s) then boiled or left to steep for the appropriate amount of time and then further substances added to improve the properties of the liquid as required.

Herbs also have a part to play in the care of familiars. They can be used to attract a specific creature and help build a deeper understanding with that beast. An obvious example would be the delight of cats when confronted with catnip, but there are many other plants which are exceedingly good for caring for your furry friend. Valerian is a notable case of a herb which is attractive to many domestic animals, including dogs, cats and horses, whilst vervain has often been used to protect livestock. Rattlesnake master needs no explanation and neither does horsetail. Then there are those which are used when intending to assume a particular animal spirit form, such as oud when wishing to fly among the ravens, goosefoot being another good herb for taking on bird form.

And finally, yet another neglected use for plants is in divining the future. Most know the usual folk superstitions of finding a four leafed clover and with it good luck or knowing that spring is truly here when you can cover seven daisies with your foot, but for someone who has fully aligned themselves with the spirits of the flora in their garden, the weave of thorns in your protective fence will also reveal with them the pattern of the future, the sound of the wind through the leaves will whisper warnings in your ear and the movement of the trees in the breeze will give indications as to which way your fortunes lie. Again, there are plants which can be used to assist you in developing your ability to See, opening doors of perception which will never fully close again, although any such activity should be undertaken with great care and only after carefully researching the appropriate plants and the correct amounts to be ingested. Those who would look to this route as being quick and easy will find themselves being sorely disappointed in the long run.

Thus it will be seen that herbs have many, many uses to the wizard and will find their way into his practises in one guise or another. It is a huge subject, well outside the scope of this guide to wizardry and anyone interested in the subject would be well advised to seek out teachers beyond what can be found in books to fully understand the subtleties of this particular Art. In their own way, plants can serve as familiars just as well as any creature with blood flowing through its veins. To disregard them will result in your magick reflecting a neglected garden – shabby, without focus and looking nothing like the glory that could be achieved with regular work and attention.

Commanding Spirits

One of the reasons why it is rare for a wizard to cast spells is because there is hardly ever any need. Why bother yourself with the hit and miss nature of the so-called Craft or petition Gods notorious for their whimsy when you can simply conjure up a spirit, give them your carefully worded order and set them to do the work for you within a strictly defined frame of reference and to a timescale of your choosing?

Evocation has a bad reputation and undeservedly so. It is perceived as being advanced, requiring skills way beyond the average mortal, even amongst those who are magickally inclined and for those who have achieved these lofty heights, it is believed that whilst they might have the ability, there is no good reason for them wanting to involve themselves in something so inherently evil and dangerous. This strange notion seems to come out of a miscomprehension that when you evoke, it is not the wizard who is in control, it is the spirit, who will subsequently lead you on a Faustian ride into damnation or worse... accountancy. Absolute nonsense.

The reality is that evocation is no more or less dangerous than any other magickal practice. It does not matter what path you choose to follow; the magick will change you. Even something as innocuous as tarot can have some very alarming effects if dealt with inappropriately, but is perfectly safe if you are following tried, tested and trusted techniques. So it is when dealing with the spirits. Can it have some unforeseen, negative results? Absolutely, but the same is true of anything which has an actual effect. Just as anything which can harm also has the power to heal, so too can the spirits have a benign or malignant influence on your life, depending on how exactly you choose to deal with them and whether you are capable of fully asserting dominance over them. There are certain modern techniques, for example, which I would not recommend because although they can produce a result, this comes with some rather interesting side effects that are not particularly desirous.

So it could be argued that evocation is an advanced path, but only insofar as you need to be confidant enough in what you're doing to be able to handle your chosen target effectively. In no other magickal practice is it perhaps as important to bear in mind the maxim of the Magus and not only Know that what you are doing will work; you must be willing to Dare. As we have seen in divination, where the question you ask is all important, so it is even more important with evocation to remember that words have power but also that where there are words, there is room for interpretation. Never kid yourself that you will have put together an absolutely watertight command for a spirit – there is always space to manoeuvre and these beasties have been playing with words for millennia. They have become extremely adept at it. So before summoning anyone, even an allegedly benign being such as an angel (which in my experience, are amongst the most frightening creatures you will ever encounter), make sure that you have considered all angles, worked out specifically what you do and do not want to see happen and make sure that you word your commands carefully to encompass both sides of the equation. You may not cover all the bases, but you can come extremely close to it if you put in appropriate preparation beforehand.

Let us examine a few modern myths surrounding evocation to see whether they hold water or not. First of all, the concept that under no circumstances should you use God names when conjuring a spirit. The reason? You don't want to upset the demon. This would be bad, because then it won't do what you want it to do. No, instead, you ought to be all nice and pally and show "*respect*" so simply call up the entity and be nice to it and it will do what you command. Yet another example of how much rubbish there is floating around in the modern magickal world.

Let me make something very clear. When you are working from a grimoire, you are walking a trodden path, one which has been proven on countless occasions to work. There is a contract which binds both sides and provided you fulfil your part of the bargain (correct tools, timings, etc.), the spirit will do theirs. Each has a different method to follow, but by and large, the principles remain the same across the board, whichever one you choose to work with (and since the Goetia seems to be currently en vogue, it should be assumed that for the purposes of this chapter, this is the book under discussion). As such, you can take it as read that if you give a demon an inch, they'll take a mile and have great fun whilst so doing. Such an approach may well bring you the results you are after – but only for as long as it suits the spirit to humour you, whether it be to lull you into a false sense of security or because it is getting more out of doing what you want than playing with you, so you need to be certain that you can maintain whatever it is you have been giving it to make working with you worthwhile. As soon as the opportunity arises to throw you the biggest curve ball possible, you can be certain that it will be coming your way and you will only have yourself to blame. Under those circumstances, it is understandable why evocation is thought of as being so hazardous, but this really is the fault of the wizard (or more precisely, the dabbler), not the system. Following the techniques laid out in the book will ensure that you are protected against the fickleness of demons, leaving you only with the wording of your commands to worry about.

One suggestion I came across once was to command the spirit, not by using the divine names, but in the name of its King, on the grounds that it will want to obey Him. An interesting notion and one which is not wholly without substance. But here's the thing. If you do not already have a working relationship with that King, why on earth do you think you have the authority to command in His name? How does using a being's name to instil obedience show respect if you haven't already communicated with that entity beforehand and established that it is acceptable for you to do this? In short, how is this any different to using divine names when you are concerned about instilling the warm fuzzies in the demon of your choice? Indeed, one would need to have worked extensively in assuming that particular King's form, channelling and focusing that energy to be entirely comfortable and sure that you are able to speak with the authority of its name to the point where the demon will listen to you as its proxy.

The King has a very specific place within the ritual, the invocation of the King to be used only when the spirit has failed to show at your command. As such, it could be argued that speaking in the name of a King is actually an escalation of dominance, rather than a more polite version of the ritual. In short, messing with a tried and tested format is likely to cause you more harm than good unless you are absolutely, 100% confidant that you know exactly what you are doing and the reasoning behind each and every alteration you make. Even so, I would strongly recommend anyone wishing to work with an altered version of the Goetic ritual, familiarise themselves with the results obtained when following the grimoire to the letter before making any adaptations in order to be able to judge truly whether what you have done gives an equally valid outcome.

Conversely, there are those who will argue that if you do not work with the Judeo-Christian cosmology, you should not be working with the God names at all, because you are calling upon a God that you do not worship (or possibly don't even believe in). Let me give you my perspective. I have never been Christian but I have no problem with using the divine names as outlined in Solomonic magick (and have never experienced an angered YHWH hunting me down for taking His name in vain) because they are just that – Divine. Whilst it cannot be denied that there is a heavy Judeo-Christian influence to many of the grimoires, which is unsurprising given the culture which produced them, it is a misconception to believe that these names are therefore referring to the Christian God alone. In fact, they are not confined to any one God and transcend such notions. They are calling upon that divine spark, that essence which resides within all of us. As such, when you are using the divine names to command, you are saying "*Listen to me. Obey me. You will hearken to me because I hold within me everything I need to ensure your compliance.*" You are not hiding behind any God. You stand before your triangle and proclaim your own authority to perform the magick. Either you speak in the name of He who spake and it was done or you don't. As Crowley tells us, there is, after all, no God but Man.

There are those who claim to be practising evocation on a regular basis who use a watered down version of the system, meditating on the spirit name in advance, for example, or asking that the spirit visit them in dreams. There are those who say that they do not use a circle or a triangle, since they do not feel that they are necessary. All of these people claim to be getting results, yet some of these do not match up to accounts from those who have done the full blown variety. Something has visited them, this much is clear; and in some cases, it may well have been the spirit called. But in many instances, their description of the being answering to the chosen name does not match up to any accounts of how the demon is supposed to appear and the information given is somewhat dubious, to say the least. And as for the more dramatic abilities ascribed to the 72? Written off as exaggerated impossibilities.

So if you feel that you wish to invent your evocation technique from scratch or treat the spirits as if they are the Goddess(TM) and require nothing more than a candle lit in their honour at regular intervals, by all means, go ahead. But be very certain in your reasons for turning your back on centuries of established magickal tradition. If it is only that you have looked at the list of required tools and believe that they are outside of your reach (lion-skin belts being somewhat hard to come by these days), take on board the fact that with a little common sense and ingenuity, there is nothing cited that cannot be relatively easily and affordably obtained or substituted. If that is all that is holding you back, then that is no excuse.

There is also more latitude in the traditional approach than might appear at first glance. It is not always necessary to evoke beings into physical presence. Astral evocation in many cases does the job just as well. It is more than acceptable to use a scrying mirror or a large piece of obsidian to conjure your spirit into, for example, allowing you to converse with it freely at length and indeed you may wish to start off with this approach and work your way up to physical presence, especially if you are concerned about "noxious breath."

There is one spirit in particular that I wish to focus on for a moment. Viné. He is the Forty-fifth Spirit of the Goetia and is a Great King and an Earl. He appears in the shape of a lion riding upon a black horse, and holding a viper in his hand. His powers are to discover things hidden, witches, **wizards**, and things present, past, and to come. **He can build towers**, overthrow great stone walls, and make the waters rough with storms. The emphasis is mine to demonstrate just how useful this fellow can be to any aspiring wizard. Feeling alone and solitary? Ask Viné to introduce you to your peers and you will soon find that you are not alone in this world. Feeling like you have not done enough work on your tower? Viné will help you achieve the lofty heights you desire. Viné is a friend to all wizards and a spirit that all wizards should converse with at some point during their magickal career. Indeed, you can use him to assist you in deciding what the next step in your magickal development should be or opening the doors to lodges previously unseen.

It should by now be apparent not only why evocation is so useful, but why it is a core practice for any wizard. It is understandable, given the myths about it, why someone would approach it with trepidation, but if you have properly prepared yourself and your working space, there is no reason for fear. It is not for nothing that you "*Dare*" to do this. If you have mastered the art of phrasing appropriate questions (as discussed in the chapter on divination), then you will be in a strong position to be in control of whatever it is you look to the spirits to provide you with, whether it be information, improved abilities or physical manifestations of your desires. Whilst the spirits are tied to their particular specialties, if you have chosen the correct one for the task at hand, the only constraint beyond that is yourself and the restrictions you place on yourself. There are no limits to what can be achieved.

Correspondences

The question of correspondences is a huge one and there are books full of lists of associations and cross-associations. As such, it would be pointless to recreate them here, when the information is so freely available. However, it is worth taking a moment to look at what they are and why they play such an important role in the art of magick.

It is not for nothing that magick is referred to as both an art and a science. There are tried and tested methods to achieve any goal and whilst we all have our own personal associations tied to colours, seasons, numbers, etc., the simple truth is that over the millennia, the more people have worked magick according to any particular system, the more that path becomes well worn and embedded, not just in our psyche, but in the universe at large. We might not understand the reasons behind why we throw spilled salt over our left shoulder (it is to chase away the devil on that side, the angel hovering over our right) or why we clink glasses before tasting our first sip of an alcoholic beverage (again, chasing away any evil spirits floating around the glass), but we know on some level that what we are doing is having an effect. So it is with the issue of correspondences. Of course, there will be occasions when you need to perform magick **now**, in which case you do the best you can given the circumstances, but if you are looking to provide your Work with that extra oomph, you will want to ensure that everything is as favourable as possible before letting loose your Will.

When you are beginning to understand correspondences and how they work, chances are that you will have piles of books strewn about the first few times, taking material, cross referencing, double checking et al - then you do it, take notes, do it again, more notes and after a while you find that it becomes second nature. You assimilate it into your practises and may even eventually find that what you are doing is not what you read in the books – but then they are inherently problematic, since it is not uncommon to find contradictions, omissions or even deliberate mistakes put there to trip up the unwary who would rather read and sound knowledgeable than attempt to put what they have learned into practise. There is also the danger of tying yourself up in knots. There is such a thing as too much information and you may well be better off starting off working within one established system and building from there. The essence of it we arrive at in our own time and flesh out the skeleton of our own accord.

If we look at some of the subjects that have been discussed in other chapters, it is immediately apparent that correspondences have an impact across the board. It is more than a mere question of associating a particular element with a certain direction of the compass (which in itself is open to debate, for example, if we look at Wiccan associations and compare those with the ones found in many Ceremonial rituals); we are looking at time of day, necessary tools, incense, deities, angels, demons, colours, etc., etc., etc. If you are planning on performing Goetic ritual, not only do you need to ensure that you are doing so on an even day of the waxing moon, but also at the right time of day depending on the spirit and that you are using an appropriate metal for your sigil and so on. It is possible to evoke ignoring these rules, but you run the risk of lessening either the results obtained, your control over the spirit or both.

We can also find correspondences having an impact on our divinatory practises – one of the reasons why astrology is highly recommended is because it contains so much information about how everything fits together and what is associated with a particular element, planet, etc. Likewise, a good tarot deck (by which I mean either the Rider Waite deck or Crowley's Thoth cards) contains information on numerology, the elements and their associated tools, the zodiac, and so on. One of the reasons why these systems work so well on anyone is that they speak to that part of us that recognises these patterns and their meaning. To attempt to piece together a magickal working ignoring or deliberately going against these traditional associations would be like attempting to swim against the tide when it is at its fiercest. Not entirely impossible, but extremely difficult and much harder work than simply waiting until you can go with the flow.

Final Words

And so to the end. Such a small book for such a big subject. Yet the reality of wizardry lies in the doing. I could have taken each topic discussed and laid out in the tiniest detail what exactly you need to be practising in order to master it and still it would mean nothing if you did not take the techniques and perform them on a regular, daily basis. Start from the moment you turn the last page. Decide that you will dedicate yourself to studying everything there is to know about each skill and put each theory to the test. Begin with the first chapter and investigate the history of wizards in greater depth. Learn all you can about the greats, the kind of people they were and the miracles they were supposed to have performed and having discovered as much as possible about the kind of person you aspire to be, move on to assembling your tools and work your way through each chapter, discerning what you need to do in order to master each area and then getting on with it. Do not simply decide in advance what will work or how things must be; learn from experimenting and realise that it is perfectly acceptable to make mistakes, as long as you learn from them. Each experience you have is a lesson in and of itself.

For it is only through experience that you can truly understand what it is I have been trying to explain with mere words. If you are lucky, you may well be able to find yourself a mentor, someone able to guide you through the twists, turns and blind alleys of a magickal life. However, whilst such a teacher is worth more than their weight in gold, they are not essential. With the application of a little common sense, a willingness to work and a commitment to walking the path, you will eventually arrive at your destination, perhaps a little frazzled from the journey, a bit frayed round the edges where you have worn away the parts of you unsuited to the honour of the title of '*wizard,*' but nevertheless, you will get there and take your place standing alongside those other rare individuals who have proven themselves worthy to hold such high office.

Further Reading & Bibliography

777 & Other Qabalistic Writings of Aleister Crowley, Aleister Crowley & Israel Regardie

A Modern Herbal, Mrs M Grieve

A Symbolic Representation of the Universe: Derived by Dr John Dee Through the Scrying of Sir Edward Kelly, Aleister Crowley & Adrian Axwirthy

Crystal-Gazing: A Study in the History, Distribution, Theory and Practice of Scrying, Theodore Besterman

Exploring the World of Lucid Dreaming, Stephen LaBerge & Howard Rheingold

First Steps in Ritual, Dolores Ashcroft-Nowicki

How to Meditate, Paul Roland

Inner Planets: Building Blocks of Personal Reality, Liz Greene

Journeys out of the Body, Robert A Monroe

Lies! Lies! Lies! The Psychology of Deceit, Charles V Ford

Magic and Showmanship, Henning Nelms

Magical Use of Thought Forms, Dolores Ashcroft-Nowicki & J H Brennan

Magick Without Peers, David Rankine & Ariadne Rainbird

Mind Magic, Marc Lemezma

Parker's Astrology: The Essential Guide to Using Astrology in Your Daily Life , Julia & Derek Parker

Planets in Transit: Life Cycles for Living, Robert Hand

Prophecy for Profit: The Essential Career and Business Guide for Those Who Give Readings, Sasha Fenton & Jan Budkowski

Psychic Self Defense, Dion Fortune

Reading People, Jo-Ellan Dimitrius

Scrying for Beginners: Tapping into the Supersensory Powers of your Subconscious, Donald Tyson

Self-Working Mental Magic, Karl Fulves

Summoning Spirits, Konstantinos

Techniques of High Magic, Francis King & Stephen Skinner

The Art of Memory, Frances A Yates

The Goetia (Lemegeton)

The Magus, Francis Barrett

The Old Testament

The Outer Planets and Their Cycles: The Astrology of the Collective, Liz Greene

The Psychology of the Psychic, David Marks

The Three Books of Occult Philosophy, Heinrich Cornelius Agrippa Von Nettesheim

Virid Arium Umbris, Daniel Schulke

Printed in the United Kingdom
by Lightning Source UK Ltd.
123883UK00002B/163-180/A

9 781905 297139